Freddy and Frankie are
two frogs who go on a journey to
Frogton where they hope to
meet the king...

A Froggy Holiday

A Bedtime Story

by George Gilfillan
illustrated by Gill Guile

Copyright © 1991 by World International Publishing Limited.
All rights reserved.
Published in Great Britain by World International Publishing Limited,
An Egmont Company, Egmont House, P.O.Box 111,
Great Ducie Street, Manchester M60 3BL.
Printed in DDR. ISBN 0 7498 0068 2

A CIP catalogue record for this book is available from the British Library

"Hooray!" cried Freddy Frog as he jumped out of bed. "It's a holiday today! I must think of something very special to do."

Freddy thought for a while. Then he croaked to himself, "I know what I'll do. I'll go to Frogton. I'll look at the king's palace and all the fine shops in the town."

So after his breakfast, Freddy Frog hopped off to Frogton.

On the way there he came across a notice which he had never seen before.

A tall, thin frog was standing by the notice. He said to Freddy, "Hello, my name is Frankie. I was on my way to Frogitch-in-the-Forest, but I read this notice and now I've changed my mind."

Freddy read the notice out loud. It was from the king and it said:

GOOD DEED WEEK
The frog who does the best good deed this week will be made a member of the Fabulous Frogs Club.

"I want to be a Fabulous Frog," said Frankie. "Then I'll be allowed to swim in the palace pond."

"And I want to be a Fabulous Frog, too," croaked Freddy.

"The best place to do a good deed is in front of the king's palace," said Frankie. "He couldn't miss seeing it then!"

"But that's not fair," Freddy said after a short while.

Then Freddy started to hop along the path which went to Frogton and Frankie followed him.

The path was so narrow that Freddy had to go first, all the way.

Shortly, they came to another notice. This one said:

DANGER!
Please keep to the path.

"Don't pay any attention," shouted Frankie. "It's just to stop frogs having picnics in the grass."

"How do you know that?" asked Freddy, curiously.

"Help!" came the faint reply.

Freddy looked around. He couldn't see Frankie anywhere. "He must have hopped off the path," said Freddy, quietly to himself.

"Help!" croaked Frankie for the second time.

"Where are you?" called Freddy.

"I'm down here," said Frankie.

He was at the bottom of a very deep hole.

"How did you get down there?" asked Freddy.

"I hopped off the path and fell in," replied Frankie, miserably.

"Aren't you going to jump out of that hole?" asked Freddy.

"I've tried. But the hole's too deep so now I'm stuck here!" said Frankie. "Do something, please!"

Freddy thought for a moment. Then he said, "That looks like the sort of hole where snakes might live...and snakes eat frogs!"

This made Frankie so frightened that he made an extra big jump.

Freddy just managed to catch Frankie by the front legs and he pulled him to safety.

They had spent so much time at the hole that now it was getting dark. So they hopped along faster than before.

"Are you sure you know the way in the dark?" grumbled Frankie.

"Of course!" said Freddy. "We're going to Frogger-on-the-Froggle to cross over the river. That's where we'll spend the night."

When they reached the village they met an old frog. He told them they could stay at Frisky Frog Farm for the night.

At Frisky Frog Farm lived old Charlie Croak. Freddy and Frankie told him that they wanted to cross the River Froggle.

"You won't be able to do that," croaked Charlie.

"Why not?" asked Freddy.

"Part of the bridge has been washed away," explained Charlie.

"Then how will we get to Frogton?" asked Frankie.

"By swimming down the river to Frog's Frolic. You can jump to the other side there," said Charlie.

When Charlie had gone, Freddy said, "We must stay here and help these poor frogs. We must mend their bridge for them."

"You can do what you like," replied Frankie, rudely. "I'm still going to Frogton to become a Fabulous Frog."

So in the morning Freddy and Frankie parted company. Frankie swam down the River Froggle towards Frog's Frolic while Freddy stayed behind to mend the broken bridge at Frogger-on-the-Froggle.

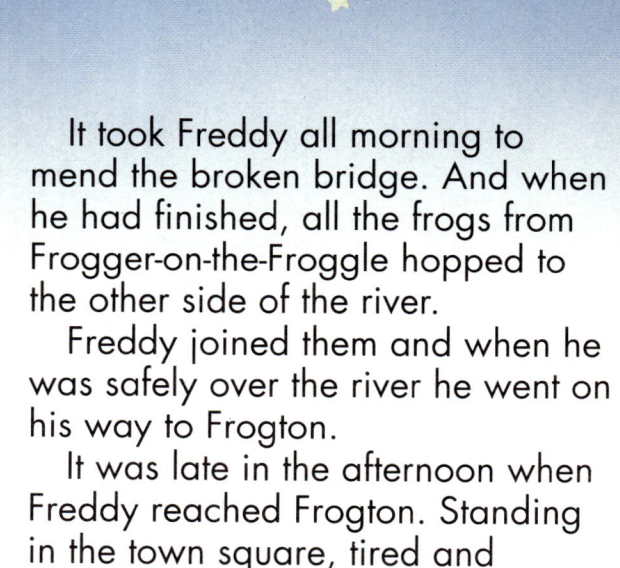

It took Freddy all morning to mend the broken bridge. And when he had finished, all the frogs from Frogger-on-the-Froggle hopped to the other side of the river.

Freddy joined them and when he was safely over the river he went on his way to Frogton.

It was late in the afternoon when Freddy reached Frogton. Standing in the town square, tired and exhausted, was Frankie.

"It's too late to do a good deed now," grumbled Frankie.

"Never mind," said Freddy. "Let's enjoy ourselves now we've come all this way." So off they hopped.

It was getting dark when a policefrog hopped up to them. "Is your name Freddy?" he asked, looking straight at Freddy.

"Er...yes, it is," Freddy replied.

"Well come along with me, young fellow," said the policefrog.

Freddy thought he was going to the police station, but instead he followed the policefrog to the kings's palace.

Inside the palace were all the frogs from Frogger-on-the-Froggle.

"That's him your majesty! That's Freddy!" they shouted.

"Come forward," called the king. Frankie stayed with the other frogs while Freddy went to the king.

"Well done, Freddy," said the king. "You are indeed a fabulous frog. I have heard that you mended the bridge over the river. That's the best deed this week!"

"Three croaks for Freddy!" they all cried. "Croak! Croak! Croak!"